THE CIVIL WAR
AND RECONSTRUCTION
A HISTORY OF BLACK PEOPLE IN AMERICA
1830-1880

Written by:
Stuart Kallen

THE CIVIL WAR AND RECONSTRUCTION
A History of Black People in America 1830-1880

Published by Abdo & Daughters, 4940 Viking Dr., Suite 622, Edina, Minnesota 55435

Library bound edition distributed by Rockbottom Books, Pentagon Tower, P.O. Box 36036, Minneapolis, Minnesota 55435

Library of Congress Number: 90-083617   ISBN: 1-56239-018-X

Cover Illustrations by: Marlene Kallen
Inside Photos by: Bettmann Archive

Reprinted 1993 by Abdo & Daughters.

Cover Illustrations by: Marlene Kallen

Edited by: Rosemary Wallner

TABLE OF CONTENTS

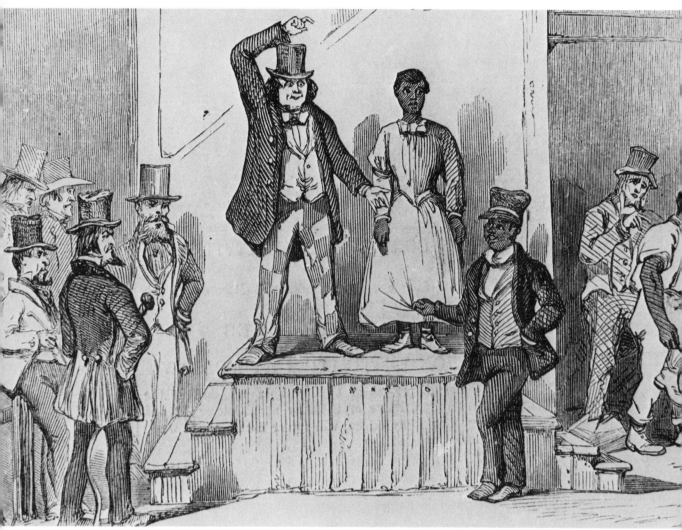

A Slave Auction

4

CHAPTER 1
A NATION DIVIDED

In 1807, the United States followed England's example and outlawed the international trading of slaves. Although the law made the importation of slaves illegal, government officials did nothing to stop it. Slave smugglers took advantage of the unguarded coastline in the southern and eastern United States and the slave trade kept growing. American sailors continued kidnapping blacks in Africa and selling them in the United States right up to the time of the Civil War.

Most of the people who wanted to stop the importation of slaves were American slave dealers. They knew that slave prices would rise if no new slaves were brought into the country. Slave trading was a big business, and Washington, D.C., was the heart of the United States slave market. Slave caravans, slave pens, and auction blocks were a common sight in the nation's capital and in other Southern cities.

Although importing of slaves was officially stopped in 1808, the number of slaves in the United States continued to grow. In 1808, about one million slaves lived in the United States. By 1861, and the start of the Civil War, over four million slaves lived in the United States. In some parts of the South, blacks outnumbered whites two to one. Almost half of the country's black population lived in Georgia, Alabama, Tennessee, Mississippi, Arkansas, Louisiana, and Texas. By 1860, slavery had been an institution in America for over 240 years.

Slave Codes

Slaves were a special kind of property as far as the law was concerned. By 1860, two sets of laws existed. One set applied to whites and the other applied to blacks, who were considered property. Slaves could not own property, be legally married, strike a white person, or possess guns. Slaves were not allowed to read or write. The state of Mississippi went as far as saying that no slave was allowed to beat a drum or blow a horn. The Constitution did not apply to slaves and free blacks. Many people felt that slave laws made a mockery of the idea that all men are created equal.

Free Blacks

Out of the four million blacks in the United States, over 500,000 were free. But many states made it difficult for free blacks to make a living. In Maryland, a special license was needed by black people who wanted to sell corn, tobacco, or wheat. Blacks were not allowed to enter the state of Indiana. Free blacks in the South had to carry "free papers" that were issued by the courts. The papers had to be renewed every so often, and the free blacks were charged a fee for this service. A person found without free papers could be jailed, hired out for work, or sold.

Free black people were not allowed to cross state borders. Free blacks who tried to enter Maryland were fined 20 dollars and refused entry. If they tried again, they were fined 500 dollars. If they could not pay, they were sold into slavery. Blacks were not allowed in restaurants or on public transportation. They were also denied the right to vote in many states. In every city in the United States, blacks were discriminated against in many ways.

Even though it was illegal in many states to teach blacks to read and write, many states had secret, underground schools. Wealthy blacks contributed generously to keep these schools in operation. In all, free blacks made lives for themselves in their own communities. In big cities, they organized clubs and societies to help each other. They opened schools, churches, and businesses. Black doctors, lawyers, businessmen and shopkeepers set up their businesses. Some black people who did not like the racism in the East, became frontiersmen in the new territories in the West.

New States and Slavery

Slavery was outlawed by many state governments in the United States. But the United States was growing at a rapid rate. The Louisiana Purchase of 1803 doubled the size of the United States. It was only a matter of time before all of the lands from Mexico to Canada and from the Atlantic to the Pacific oceans were part of the United States. When new territories became states, the debate over slavery was renewed. By 1820, eleven states approved of slavery and eleven states were against it. That meant that the United States Senate was evenly balanced. The North and the South both had twenty-two senators.

Missouri wanted to join the United States in 1820. Angry debates took place in Congress over whether Missouri should become a slave state or a free state. At the same time, Maine, which was then part of Massachusetts, also wanted to become a separate state. An agreement was made that Maine would be admitted as a free state if Missouri could be a slave state. Congress drew an imaginary line across the United States. In new states north of the line, slavery would be outlawed. Any new states south of the line would be slave states. This act was called the Missouri Compromise.

By 1850, California, New Mexico, and Utah all wanted to become states. Most Northerners did not want slavery in the new states. Most Southerners wanted slavery. For nine months, bitter debate raged in Congress over the slavery issue. Finally, the Northerners and the Southerners reached a compromise consisting of four points. First, Congress would admit California as a free state; second, it would open New Mexico and Utah as territories where slavery would be legal; third, Congress would end the slave trade in Washington, D.C.; and fourth, Congress would protect slave owners by passing strict fugitive slave laws.

The Compromise of 1850 as the four points were called, upset almost everyone. The Southern states considered seceding from, or leaving, the United States. Northerners did not want slavery in any new territories. And the fugitive slave laws upset blacks and Northerners alike.

The Fugitive Slave Law
The fugitive slave laws put the United States government in the business of catching runaway slaves. Federal officers were paid a fee for every runaway slave they returned to their owners. Soon, runaway slave catching became a profitable business.

Unfortunately, the men who made their business catching runaway slaves did not care if they were catching a free black or a runaway. Any black person was fair game. In 1850, over 500,000 free blacks lived in the North and South. But blacks could not testify in court and could not defend themselves against the federal marshalls, judges, and jailers. Many thousands of free blacks were kidnapped and taken from their homes to face a life of slavery in the South. Many escaped slaves were sent back to plantations in the South to face whippings, beatings, and even death. All this was done with United States government money paid to government agents.

Nat Turner's Rebellion

Nat Turner was a man who looked heavenward for signs. Turner was a very religious man known as "the Prophet" by the people who knew him. He preached on Sundays and had the respect of the black and white communities. But Turner felt that his life was useless as a slave. He wanted to free the black race from the chains of slavery. Turner worked in the fields in Southhampton County, Virginia, waiting for a sign from God. An eclipse of the sun occured in February 1831. Turner took the eclipse to be the sign he was waiting for. He gathered his friends together and organized a massive slave uprising on the Fourth of July. But Turner became ill and canceled his plans.

On August 13, Turner saw another sign: the sun was covered by a greenish-blue haze. Once again, Turner planned an uprising. On August 22, 1831, Turner killed his owner Joseph Travis, his wife, and two children. Two other people were also killed. Between sixty and eighty slaves went on a rampage. They killed more than fifty-eight slaveholders and their families.

News of the revolt soon reached the local sheriff, and hundreds of men picked up their guns and went searching for Turner and his men. When they found the rebels, dozens of slaves were killed. Turner avoided the police for two months, but was finally captured by the Virginia militia on October 30, 1831. Five days later he was put on trial, found guilty, and hanged.

At his trial, Turner said that the sun would refuse to shine on the day he went to the gallows. He said it would be a sign from God that slavery was evil. Many people scoffed at Turner's prediction. But the local sheriff took him seriously. The sheriff refused to cut the rope that would open the trap door on the gallows to drop Turner to his death. No one else in the county would do it either, so an old tramp who lived forty miles away was brought in to be the executioner. On the day of the hanging, a major thunderstorm darkened the sky with thick black clouds. Many people believed that this was the sign from God that Turner had spoken of.

Turner's rebellion touched off a wave of white on black violence. Seventeen men who had fought with Turner were hanged. More than 200 slaves who had nothing to do with Turner were killed in order to scare other slaves.

After two months of hiding, Nat Turner is captured by a Virginia militiaman.

Slaveholders started arming themselves. They organized militias in case another rebellion started. Strict laws were passed to further tighten the bonds of slavery in the South. Slaveholders became convinced that the whip and the gun were the only ways to control slaves. Hundreds of innocent slaves were tortured and killed.

The Abolitionist Movement

People who wanted to do away with, or abolish, slavery were called *abolitionists*. After the Revolutionary War, free blacks became more and more opposed to slavery. Many of these people had taught themselves to read and write. The abolitionists spoke and wrote about the evils of slavery. White abolitionists joined the blacks and toured the country demanding freedom for the slaves. Abolitionists talked, prayed, and preached the message of freedom.

Abolitionists were disliked by many people. One abolitionist was killed by a mob in Illinois in 1837. Many Southern post offices refused to deliver antislavery newspapers. The state of Georgia offered a 5,000 dollar reward to anyone who brought William Garrison, an abolitionist, to trial.

Many white people felt that if the slaves were freed, their jobs would be threatened. These people booed and harrassed abolitionists wherever they spoke.

William Lloyd Garrison, An American Abolitionist

The Underground Railroad

The Underground Railroad was not underground and it was not really a railroad. It was a network of black and white people who helped slaves escape to the North where they would be free. Thousands of people took part in the organization that helped runaways escape to nonslave states. After the passage of the fugitive slave laws, runaways were forced to go to Canada to flee slavery.

Conductors on the Underground Railroad led slaves along backcountry roads in the dead of night. During the day, slaves were hidden in barns, basements, or attics, far from the bloodhounds that were tracking them. Places where slaves hid were called depots or stations. Slaves were given food and clothing on the Underground Railroad. Night after night, the runaway slaves continued on their journey until they reached freedom. No one knows exactly how many people escaped slavery on the Underground Railroad, but scholars estimate that between 100,000 and 200,000 people found freedom that way. Levi Coffin, a Quaker, was called "President of the Underground Railroad." Coffin helped more than 3,000 slaves find their way to freedom.

A slave needed courage and skill to run away. One man nailed himself in a box and had himself mailed to the North. Another man walked 1,500 miles to freedom in a pair of shoes he carved out of wood. Secret information was passed along by slaves in song lyrics. The song "Follow the Drinking Gourd" referred to the stars that formed the Little Dipper. That constellation included the North Star, and was used by runaways to direct them to the North. The gospel song "Swing Low Sweet Chariot, Coming for to Carry Me Home" meant that a person from the Underground Railroad was "coming for to carry" a person "home" to freedom. The song "Wade in the Water" told runaways to travel in rivers and streams so that dogs could not track them.

Many Underground Railroad conductors were sent to jail, and some were murdered. But slaves continued to escape on the Railroad until the Civil War.

Uncle Tom's Cabin

Harriet Beecher Stowe was a white abolitionist from Cincinnati, Ohio. One day she heard about Eliza, a slave who decided to run away to Canada in the middle of the winter. Eliza and her baby escaped from a farm in Kentucky. Her journey to freedom brought her north to the Ohio River. The river was only partially frozen, and Eliza could not cross. Eliza and her baby waited through the cold winter night for the river to freeze.

Harriet Beecher Stowe, author of Uncle Tom's Cabin.

The next morning, Eliza saw slave catchers and bloodhounds coming for her. She wrapped her baby around her in a shawl and jumped. From one iceberg to the next, Eliza made her way across the icy, flowing water. In time, Eliza made her way to Canada. The following summer, she returned to Kentucky and helped her five children escape to freedom.

When Harriet Beecher Stowe heard Eliza's story, she decided to write a book about slavery and include Eliza's heroic journey. Stowe titled the book *Uncle Tom's Cabin*. She said she hoped to make enough money from the book to buy a new silk dress.

When it was published in 1851, *Uncle Tom's Cabin* became an instant best-seller. No book had ever sold so fast. Eight printing presses running night and day could not keep up with the demand for the book. Over 300,000 copies were sold in the first year. The book sold in England, France, and Germany but was banned in the South.

Uncle Tom's Cabin was based, in part, on the life of a slave named Josiah Henson. In the story, Henson described how, an angry slave owner had cut off his father's ear. When Stowe's book became a best-seller, a letter arrived in her home one day. When she opened it, out fell the ear of another slave — a threat from a plantation owner in the South.

Uncle Tom's Cabin helped many people see the evils of slavery for the first time. More and more people became abolitionists, and the nation was divided even further.

The Dred Scott Decision

Dred Scott was born a slave in Virginia around 1795. His owner died in 1831, and he was sold to John Emerson, an Army surgeon. Emerson moved to Illinois. He believed that he could own a slave there even though Illinois was a free state because he intended to return someday to Missouri where slavery was legal. Emerson was transferred by the Army to Wisconsin, another free state. In 1839, Emerson and Scott returned to Missouri.

When Dr. Emerson died in 1843, Scott tried to purchase freedom for himself and his family from Emerson's wife. When Mrs. Emerson refused, Scott sued. He believed he should be free because of the years he spent in free territory.

Scott lost his first case but appealed to the ruling. This time he won the battle in a St. Louis courtroom. This ruling was overturned by the Missouri Supreme Court in 1852. With the help of white abolitionists, Scott appealed his case to the United States Supreme Court. Unfortunately, the chief justice of the court, Roger B. Taney, was a southerner who believed in slavery.

Dred Scott   Harriet, wife of Dred Scott.

On March 6, 1857, the Supreme Court handed down its decision. The court said that because Scott was a black man, he was not a citizen of the United States and had no right to sue anyone. The court also said that Congress could not prevent slave owners from taking their property (in this case, slaves) anywhere in the country. This meant that all antislavery laws were unconstitutional and worthless to protect blacks. Taney wrote, "Blacks are an inferior class of being and have no rights which the white man was bound to respect."

The reaction to Taney's bigotry was immediate and widespread. Meetings were held throughout the country to protest the decision. Today, many people think that the Dred Scott decision helped bring about the Civil War. People no longer felt that a peaceful solution to slavery was possible.

CHAPTER 2
FRIENDS OF FREEDOM —
ENEMIES OF SLAVERY

John Copeland, Jr. - 1836-1859
Fighter of Freedom

Almost everyone has heard the song words, "John Brown's body lies a-mouldering in the grave but his truth goes marching on." The song was written about a white abolitionist, John Brown, from Kansas. Brown was convinced that slavery should be ended immediately and wanted to lead a slave revolt in Virginia.

John Copeland joined up with Brown after being released from jail where he served time for helping a runaway slave. On October 16, 1859, John Brown, Copeland, and twenty-one other followers captured an armory and arsenal in Harpers Ferry, West Virginia. An alarm was sounded and soon the Virginia Militia and the U.S. Marines, led by Robert E. Lee, surrounded Brown's men at the arsenal. Dangerfield Newby, a free black man hoping to free his slave wife and children, was the first to die. Brown's two sons were shot next.

Soon, eight more men lay dead. One man, Osborn Anderson, a college student, managed to escape. John Copeland, Brown, and five others were captured. After a long trial, the men were sentenced to death.

On the evening before he was to die, Copeland wrote a letter to his parents. "I am not terrified by the gallows," Copeland wrote, "I am soon to suffer death for doing what George Washington was made a hero for doing. I am dying for freedom. I could not not die for a better cause." On December 16, 1859, John Copeland was hanged for fighting for the freedom of slaves. The execution of Copeland and John Brown's men angered abolitionists all over the country and was one of the final acts that touched off the Civil War.

Frederick Douglass - 1817-1895
Publisher

Frederick Douglass is considered the father of the ninteenth-century civil rights movement. He was a publisher, a diplomat to Haiti and the Dominican Republic, and a friend of Abraham Lincoln.

Frederick Douglass was born in Maryland in 1817 and named Frederick Bailey. His mother was a slave, and he did not know who his father was. Douglass did not know his exact birthday so he picked February 14, Valentine's Day, because his mother called him her "little valentine." Douglass's mother was sold to a plantation twelve miles away. Sometimes after work, she forced herself to walk that distance to see her son. She would spend the night and when Douglass awoke, his mother would be gone. She died when Frederick was about seven years old.

As a child, Douglass was forced to fend for himself. Like all other slave children, his only clothing was a rough, knee-length shirt. He had no shoes, jacket, or pants. Douglass was so cold in the winter that he had to use a burlap sack to stay warm. When he slept on the floor at night, he used the sack for a blanket. Many times, Douglass had to wrestle with "Old Nep," the dog, for a few scraps of food that had been thrown out.

Douglass was sent to Baltimore, Maryland, to act as a companion for his master's nephew, Tommy Auld. In Baltimore Douglass learned to read and write. When he was sixteen years old, his master's wife died and Douglass was ordered back to the plantation. One day, Douglass refused the orders of his master and was hired out to Mr. Covey, a well-known "slave breaker." Covey constantly beat and whipped Douglass. He denied him food and forced him to work fifteen hours a day. Douglass fought back as well as he could.

Later when Douglass was hired out to another farmer, he planned an escape. With five other men, Douglass planned to steal a boat and row seventy miles across Chesapeake Bay. Then the men would hike into Pennsylvania. Douglass forged "free papers," but was arrested and thrown in jail before the plan could be carried out.

Douglass was sent back to Baltimore where he worked in the shipyards. There, he met and fell in love with a free black woman named Anna Murray. Murray and Douglass plotted another escape attempt. By borrowing the papers from a friendly black sailor, Douglass was able to escape to New York City. In New York, Douglass stayed with David Ruggles, a black abolitionist. Douglass soon sent for Anna and they were married. The next day they left New York and sailed to New Bedford, Massachusetts. To avoid slave hunters, Douglass changed his last name from Baily to Douglass.

In Massachusetts, Douglass met William Loyd Garrison, publisher of the antislavery newspaper *The Liberator*. Garrison put Douglass in touch with abolitionists who wanted his services. Soon, Douglass was asked to speak at rallies. Douglass spoke so intelligently that many people began to doubt if he had ever really been a slave. To ease any doubts about his life, Douglass wrote *Narrative of the Life of Frederick Douglass, an American Slave*. Information in the book told of slaves, owners, and places where Douglass had lived. The book was so exact Douglass was afraid his old owner would find out where he lived and come after him. Douglass and Anna soon moved to England.

In England, Douglass lectured about slavery, women's rights, and world peace. His regal appearance and intelligent lectures won him many friends. Although his friends wanted him to stay in England, Douglass felt he should return to America. He wanted to help other black people out of slavery. To avoid being captured in America, Douglass's English friends purchased his freedom.

In 1847, Douglass settled in Rochester, New York, and started a newspaper called the *North Star*. The paper was named after the North Star in the Little Dipper. In his paper, Douglass wrote of the evils of slavery and called for equal rights for Native Americans and women. In 1848, Douglass met John Brown. Later, when Brown was arrested for raiding the Virginia arsenal, the governor of Virginia accused Douglass of helping plan the raid and issued a warrant for his arrest. Douglass was forced to flee to Canada where he remained until 1860.

When the Civil War started in 1861, Douglass urged President Lincoln to free all the slaves and allow them to join the army. Shortly afterward, Lincoln issued the Emancipation Proclamation that did what Douglass asked. Douglass started the all-black Fifty-fourth and Fifty-fifth Massachusetts regiments. His two sons were the first to enlist.

For the next fifteen years, Douglass was appointed to government posts by several presidents. Douglass was the marshall of the District of Columbia, recorder of deeds, and diplomat to Haiti and the Dominican Republic. After retiring, Douglass focused on the problems of discrimination and murder of blacks in the

Frederick Douglass welcomes visitors to his newspaper office.

South. On February 20, 1895, Frederick Douglass died of a heart attack.

Douglass was a great writer, political analyst, diplomat, and speaker. He advanced the cause of freedom and liberty for blacks and whites alike. He is remembered to this day as the greatest black leader of the 1800's.

Harriet Tubman - 1821-1913
Conductor on the Underground Railroad

Harriet Tubman was perhaps the most famous conductor on the Underground Railroad. Slave owners were so afraid of her that they offered a reward of 40,000 dollars to anyone who captured her, dead or alive. Her philosophy is summed up in her quote, "You'll be free or die. There is [sic] two things I have a right to, liberty or death. If I could not have one, I would have the other. For no man shall take me alive." No one ever did capture Tubman. For sixteen years, she made nineteen dangerous trips to the South to bring over 300 slaves to freedom (including her elderly parents). Tubman never lost one slave in her journey.

Tubman was born in 1821 in Dorchester County, Maryland. She was a highly intelligent child in a family of eleven children. Tubman was not allowed to learn to read and write and spent her childhood working the fields. When she was sixteen years old she tried to protect another slave who was being beaten by an angry overseer. Her master threw a rock at her and the blow almost killed her. For the rest of her ninty-two years, Tubman suffered seizures and blackouts from that incident. Soon after, Tubman began to hear voices and see visions warning her of danger and telling her to escape.

When Tubman was twenty-eight years old, she followed the North Star to freedom in Philadelphia, Pennsylvania. Soon she joined the Underground Railroad and made her first journey to help runaway slaves. In between rescue missions, she worked as a cook and laundry washer to earn money. When she had earned enough for a rescue mission, she would disguise herself and make her way south into slave territory.

Harriet Tubman (left, holding a pan) photographed with a group of slaves that she had led to freedom.

When Tubman passed white people in her disguise, they saw a half-crazed, harmless old woman singing gospel songs. What the people did not know was that the songs were sung in code to alert slaves of her arrival. Once the slaves decided to join her, they had to follow Tubman's strict rules. Be on time, tell no one of your plan, follow all orders, and be prepared to die before you turn back. Tubman carried a gun and threatened to shoot anyone who turned back. No one ever did.

To get a jump on the slave owners, Tubman always planned her escapes for Saturday night. That way, slave owners could not print reward notices until Monday morning. This gave the slaves a thirty-six-hour head start.

During the Civil War, Tubman worked as a scout and spy for the Union Army. On one raid, she freed over 750 slaves. After the war, Tubman organized schools for black children and spoke for women's rights. When Tubman died in 1913, she was buried in Ohio with military honors. Flags flew at half-mast and blacks and whites alike gathered to pay tribute to the brave conductor on the Underground Railroad. In 1978, the U.S. Postal Service issued a stamp honoring Tubman.

Jermain Wesley Loguen - 1813-1872
Conductor on the Underground Railroad

Harriet Tubman helped over 300 people escape slavery, but she would not have been able to do it if she had not gained her own freedom. The man that helped her was Jermain Wesley Loguen.

Jermain Loguen was born near Nashville, Tennessee. His mother was a free black woman who was kidnapped and sold to a man named David Logue. Logue became Jermain's father, but Logue cared nothing for him. David Logue soon sold Jermain and his mother. Logue's mother had a baby daughter who was sold as an infant. Jermain saw the suffering of his mother and decided to run away.

Logue escaped to Canada where he went to school. Later he moved to New York and opened several schools for black children. In 1842 he became a minister and opened five churches. Sometime during this period he changed his name to Loguen.

Loguen worked with Frederick Douglass on the *North Star* and became a conductor on the Underground Railroad. During his lifetime he helped Harriet Tubman and over 1,500 other slaves escape on the "Freedom Train."

Sojourner Truth - 1797-1883
Abolitionist, Preacher,
Women's Rights Activist

Sojourner Truth was born Isabella Baumfree in Hurley, New York, in 1797. Truth suffered terrible cruelties living the life of a slave. She had thirteen children and saw most of them sold into slavery. She was sold four times and finally ran away only one year before slavery was officially ended in New York in 1826. A Quaker family helped her win a lawsuit to have one of her children returned to her. The child had been sold when he was five years old to a slave owner in Alabama.

Truth worked in New York and attended several churches. In 1843, she said a voice from God came to her and told her to change her name to Sojourner. The voice also told her to travel "up and down the land showing people their sins." Sojourner asked God for a second name and he told her "Truth," because she was to tell everyone the truth about slavery.

For twenty years, Truth traveled around the country speaking about slavery and women's rights. She had a deep, booming voice, and her speeches won her the respect of many abolitionists. She was even invited to the White House to meet with Abraham Lincoln. During the Civil War, Truth raised money for black Union soldiers by lecturing and singing. She became so famous that books were written about her even though Truth herself could not read. After the Civil War, Truth tried to obtain land out West for the newly freed slaves.

CHAPTER 3
THE CIVIL WAR

Abraham Lincoln

Many events in the 1850's led to great disagreements between the North and South. When Abraham Lincoln was elected President of the United States in 1860, the rift turned to war. Lincoln was a member of the Republican Party that had been formed in 1854. Republicans were against the expansion of slavery into any new states. Lincoln believed in his party's position on slavery, but denied that he would free the slaves. He promised he would enforce the Fugitive Slave Law and allow slavery to continue where it already existed.

Abraham Lincoln

The Southerners did not believe Lincoln. They did believe any state could leave the Union if they chose to. On December 20, 1860, South Carolina became the first state to secede from, or leave, the Union. By the time Lincoln was sworn in as President in January 1861, Mississippi, Georgia, Florida, Tennessee, Louisiana, and Alabama had seceded also.

On February 4, 1861, representatives of the seven seceded states met in Montgomery, Alabama. They named their new country the Confederate States of America. On April 12, 1861, Confederate soldiers attacked Union soldiers at Fort Sumter, South Carolina, and the Civil War began.

Blacks Not Allowed

The Civil War quickly turned into a bloody nightmare for the North and South. New weapons killed hundreds of thousands of soldiers but there was no modern medicine to heal the wounded. Blacks, however, were quite ready to do battle for freedom and the Union. "Men of color, to arm!" wrote Frederick Douglass. Black men, slave and free, rushed to join up with the Union Army. In Philadelphia, a group came up with a plan for organizing slave revolts in the South. Slaves left plantations by the thousands to help the cause.

The Civil War began in 1861 and lasted for four long years.

A field hospital in Virginia during the Civil War.

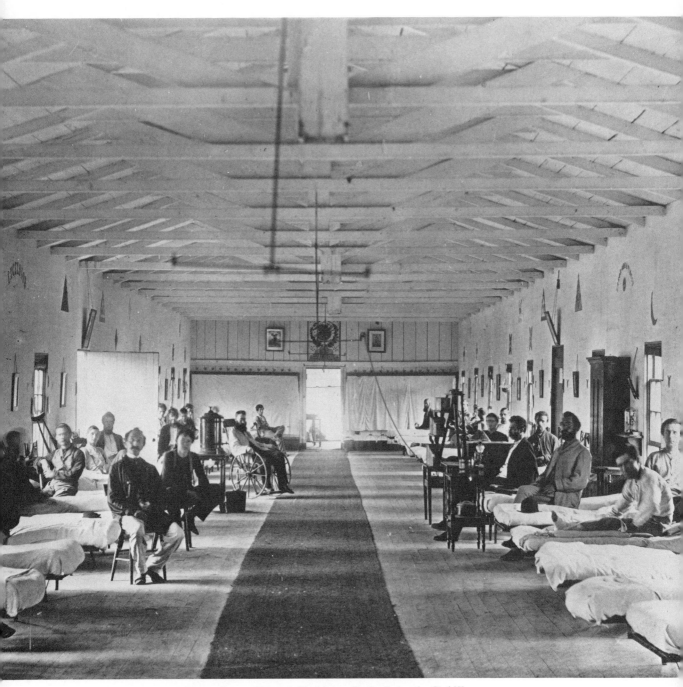

Amory Square Hospital, Washington D. C., during the Civil War.

Free blacks in cities like Boston and New York, at their own expense, organized and drilled regiments.

But the Union did not want the blacks to fight. The War Department was afraid that whites would not fight alongside black troops. And Lincoln stated that the Civil War was to reunite the country not to free the slaves. Lincoln said, "If I could save the Union without freeing any slaves, I would do it; and if I could save it by freeing all the slaves I would do it; and if I could save it by freeing some and leaving others alone I would also do that." Also, Lincoln did not want to anger border states that had not left the Union. In Union states like Kentucky, slavery was still legal. In fact, during the early days of the war, Union soldiers were instructed to return runaway slaves to their owners.

The Emancipation Proclamation

On January 1, 1863, Lincoln signed the Emancipation Proclamation. (To emancipate someone means to set them free.) The Emancipation Proclamation declared that all slaves in the Confederate States were free.

The proclamation did not apply to slaves behind Union lines. Maryland, Delaware, Kentucky, and Missouri were Union states where slavery was still legal. Therefore, Lincoln had freed the slaves in the Confederate states where he did not really have the power to do so. But he had not freed the 800,000 slaves in the Union where he did have the power.

Despite this problem, the Emancipation Proclamation set wheels in motion to end slavery in the United States. Slaves started running away in record numbers. The whole institution of slavery started falling apart. Finally, the federal government supported freedom for all people, regardless of their race.

In 1865, Congress passed the Thirteenth Amendment to the Constitution. The Amendment made slavery illegal everywhere in the United States. After two-and-a-half centuries of government-sanctioned human bondage, slavery was finally abolished.

Black Soldiers in the Civil War

During the first year of the Civil War, black participation was limited to helping white soldiers behind the lines. Blacks worked as horse drivers, cooks, blacksmiths, construction workers, waiters, and helpers. Many white soldiers disagreed with Lincoln's slave policy of keeping out blacks. One general in South Carolina tried to arm thousands of runaway slaves but was stopped. General Ben Butler declared runaway slaves "contraband," which means illegal goods. Butler ordered the "contraband" freed, and within two months, 900 blacks were working for the Union Army.

After the signing of the Emancipation Proclamation, black men signed up for the Union Army in huge numbers. By the end of 1863, over 50,000 black soldiers were fighting in the Civil War. In all, over 200,000 blacks fought for the Union army and navy. Another 200,000 black men and women worked as scouts, nurses, guides, spies, cooks, and laborers. An unknown number of slaves were forced to fight for the Confederate Army.

B-250

The Life of a Black Soldier

Blacks were discriminated against even in the war. Blacks who fought for the Union army only received ten dollars a month while white soldiers received thirteen dollars a month. Much of their equipment was faulty goods that white soldiers had thrown away. A worse fate awaited black soldiers who were captured by the Confederates. Sometimes the captured soldiers were sold into slavery, sometimes they were just murdered in cold blood. In 1864, over 300 black soldiers were massacred when they were forced to surrender at Fort Pillow, Tennessee. Six days later, wounded and captured soldiers were murdered by Confederate troops in Arkansas.

Lincoln issued an order stating that for every black prisoner shot, a Confederate prisoner would be killed. And for every black soldier sold into slavery, a Confederate prisoner would be subjected to forced labor. Blacks fought fiercely, willing to die before surrendering.

By the end of the war, twenty black soldiers had received the nation's highest honor, The Congressional Medal of Honor. But blacks paid a high price in the Civil War. Over 68,000 men died, or one out of every five who had fought. Thousands more were wounded.

47

After four bloody years, the Civil War finally ended on April 9, 1865. The North had won the war but the whole country had paid heavily to end slavery and preserve the Union. One out of every five Americans was killed in the Civil War — 600,000 people. The South was in ruins and millions of Southerners were homeless and starving. Millions of blacks with no skills, no homes, and nowhere to go were suddenly free. Many of these people could not read or write. The freed blacks looked to the United States government for help.

Reconstruction

In March 1865, the federal government set up the Freedman's Bureau. It was run by the U.S. Army. People in the South were strongly opposed to the Freedman's Bureau. They still resisted equality for black people. The bureau tried to find homes and jobs for former slaves, provide them with medicine and health care, and protect them from unfair labor practices. The bureau built over 4,000 schools, which eventually educated 250,000 black people.

White politicians in the South passed "Black Codes" that barred blacks from voting and prevented them from getting jobs and using public areas. To counter this, Congress passed the Reconstruction Act of 1867, the act put ten southern states under military law. Congress also passed the Fourteenth and Fifteenth amendments to the Constitution. The Fourteenth Amendment guaranteed equal rights for every person regardless of race. The Fifteenth Amendment guaranteed black men the right to vote. Other civil rights acts made it illegal to keep blacks out of hotels, theaters, railroads, and other public places.

The new rights mobilized large numbers of blacks in the South to vote. Many blacks were elected to state and federal governments. Mississippi sent three black men to the United States Congress. South Carolina sent two. In all, over twenty black men served in Congress before 1900. The black legislatures enacted new laws guaranteeing free public education for blacks. Other laws abolished common criminal punishments like branding and whipping. Blacks were also elected as governors, judges, and other posts. These men brought many good ideas to state and local governments,

Many laws of the nineteenth century that were passed by blacks are still in effect today.

The White Resistance

Many Southern whites were violently opposed to black people voting or owning land. Secret organizations were formed by Civil War veterans to terrorize black people from exercising their rights. The groups had names like the White Brotherhood, the Rifle Clubs, the Palefaces, and the Knights of the White Camellia. The Ku Klux Klan was the largest and most violent group.

A visit by the Ku Klux Klan.

The Ku Klux Klan in costume.

A black man killed by the Ku Klux Klan.

Its members dressed in masks and sheets and were supposed to look like dead Confederate soldiers who had risen from the grave. They used whips, guns, fire, and lynchings to kill innocent black men, women, and children.

In 1877, Reconstruction offically ended and federal troops were removed from the South. Once again blacks were left to fend for themselves in the South. Without federal protection, blacks were quickly pushed aside by the white power structure. Thousands of blacks were killed by white terrorists. Homes, schools, and farms were burned. The Ku Klux Klan's terrorism eventually pushed blacks out of voting and out of government. By 1901, people had voted out all the blacks in the United States Congress. New laws were passed by whites in the South called "Jim Crow" laws. The laws prevented blacks from using public transportation, theaters, and restaurants. Many of these Jim Crow laws were in effect in the South for the next one hundred years.

CHAPTER 4
REBUILDERS OF HOPE

Robert Smalls - 1839-1915
Civil War Hero, Congressman

When Robert Smalls was twenty-three years old, he became a very big man. On May 13, 1862, Smalls, a slave, crept aboard a Confederate ship called the *Planter* that was anchored in the harbor at Charleston, South Carolina. The *Planter's* crew had gone ashore for the night. Smalls, his wife, children, and five other people hoisted the Confederate flag and sailed the ship into the open seas. The hijackers needed the Confederate flag so that the ship could safely pass the well-armed Fort Sumter.

The soldiers that saw the *Planter* pass saw Smalls with a large straw hat pulled over his face. They thought he was the ship's captain. When Smalls reached Union waters, he hauled down the Confederate flag and hoisted a white truce flag. Then Smalls and the crew turned the ship over to the Union Navy.

The story of the hijacked ship soon made Smalls a well-known man. President Lincoln awarded Smalls 1,500 dollars for the ship. He was made a commander in the Union Navy and piloted the *Planter* until after the war.

When Smalls retired from the Navy, he was elected to the South Carolina House of Representatives. Later he was elected to the United States Congress. While in office, Smalls worked to pass laws to promote black education. Smalls was never intimidated by white terrorists. In 1913, he single-handedly stopped two black men from being lynched by a mob in South Carolina. He was seventy-three years old at the time.

Booker T. Washington 1856-1915
Educator

In 1865, the Civil War ended. That was also the year that Booker T. Washington turned nine years old. Washington did not get to play like the other children. He had to get out of bed at 4 a.m. to work in the salt mines in Malden, West Virginia. At night, after his sixteen-hour shift, Washington taught himself to read.

In 1872, Washington left home to attend an agricultural college in Virginia. Washington did not have money to travel, so he walked across West Virginia to get to the school. Washington was lucky, a white friend paid for his tuition. At his commencement, Washington graduated with honors and gave a speech.

In 1881, the state of Alabama decided to build a school in Tuskegee to train black teachers. Washington's college suggested that he be the dean of the new school. Washington was determined to make the new school a success.

Booker T. Washington (seated left front) and a group of associates at the Tuskegee Insitute.

58

He bought an abandoned plantation and turned it into a college. Students built classrooms, a chapel, and dormitories. They learned farming, carpentry, shoemaking, and printing.

In four years, Tuskegee Institute became the leading black school in the United States. By 1888, it had over 400 students. Washington's efforts to raise money for the school brought him in contact with America's top white businessmen. In 1892, Washington established the National Negro Businessmen League to help black businessmen. He also wrote *Up From Slavery*, a book about his life that became a best-seller and was sold all over the world. Washington also advised presidents Theodore Roosevelt and William Taft about political issues.

Booker T. Washington was a hard-working, self-made man. His contribution to black culture can still be felt today.

Booker T. Washington, founder of Tuskegee Institute.

A FINAL WORD

By 1880, the Civil War was over and blacks were free. But most blacks in the South found themselves in as bad a situation as they had been when they were slaves. Low paying jobs were usually the only ones open to black people. Land and supplies were expensive and blacks were forced to go into debt to landowners to keep from starving. The Civil War freed the blacks from slavery, but for many, life stayed the same. Men like Frederick Douglass and Booker T. Washington began the fight for Civil Rights. The next one hundred years would see many more changes for blacks in America.

INDEX